Marzetta Stood In For Mama

By Glenda Horton Manning

ENHEART PUBLISHING

ENHEART PUBLISHING
P. O. Box 560576
Charlotte, NC 28256-0576

Library of Congress Catalog Card Number: 99-66002

ISBN: 0-9654899-1-4

Illustrations by Duy Huynh
Design Layout by Lea'Vee L. Jordan

Printed in the United States of America

Dedication

This book is dedicated to teachers everywhere. Teaching is touching
the mind through the heart. May God bless teachers
especially those who are not afraid to touch children,
for when we touch children we touch the future.

~ A special thank you to my dear friend, JoAnne Holmes.
She is a dedicated teacher
who believes in children and the power of her touch.
~ I must also remember Daddy
my first and most important teacher.

Acknowledgements

*T*here are many, many people here unnamed who have contributed
to my growth and in some way have made this book possible.   I am grateful to all of them:
those who have taught and touched me, those who have loved and invested in me,
I thank each and all of them.

I am especially grateful to:

Robert Lee Davis, my junior high school Language Arts teacher.
Daily I use his unique words and examples of public speaking.

Barbara W. Davis, my high school English teacher who became my mentor
and continues to shape, make and mold me.

Carol Boggs, my college professor who became my personal friend and advisor.

Finally, I thank God Almighty for blessing me with a special gift and an opportunity to give.

Thanks to this Circle of Friends

Seated from left to right: Duy T. Huynh (Illustrator), Carol Dunn Gaston (Administration for Touch, Inc.),
Glenda Horton Manning (Author), Pat Schulz (Publisher), Lea'Vee L. Jordan (Graphic Designer)

Marzetta Stood In For Mama

*F*ourth grade was tough. The chairs were bigger. The reading books were harder...even the math books had word problems. Fourth grade was tough.

Being nine was tough too. For most kids being nine is hard, unless you have friends to laugh and giggle with and a mother to help you with homework. I had neither.

Mama was sick in her mind, so they took her to a special hospital many miles away. I almost never got to see her. Things were tough because I missed Mama and the things she did. Mothers do things that help make life easier for their children.

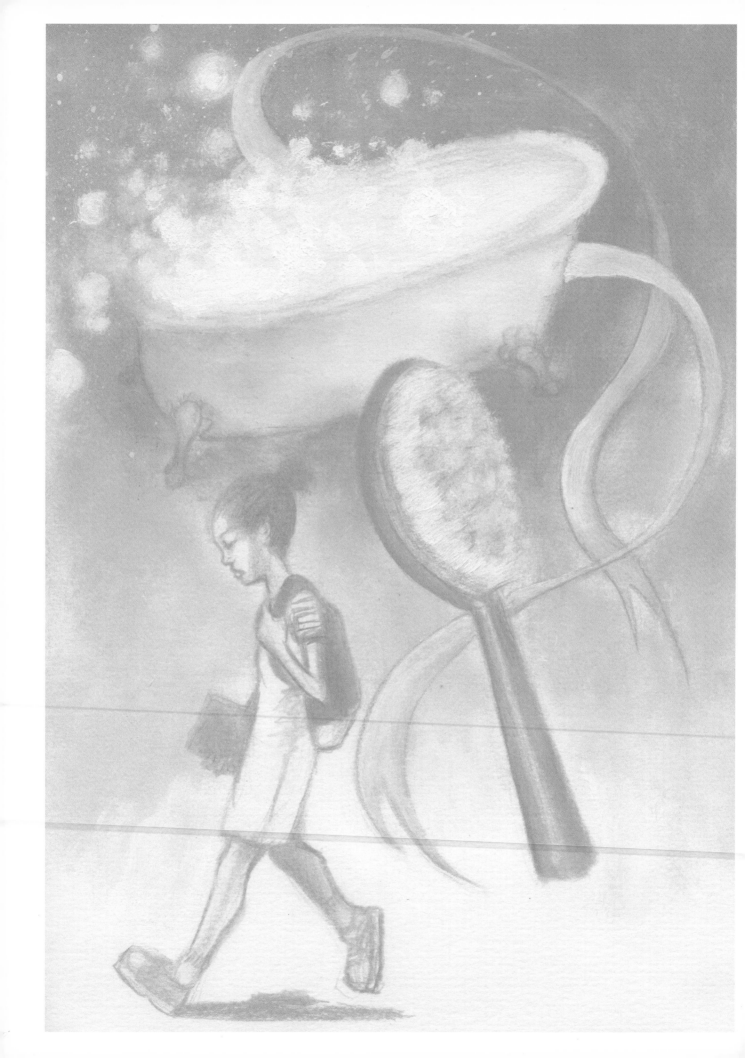

I remembered when Mama did those things. She bathed

my body and made me smell sweet. She combed

my hair then tied on a silk ribbon. She helped

with homework. She read to me. She smiled.

She hugged me. And then one day she was gone.

They said she was sick. And they took her away.

Fourth grade was tough because without Mama I

did not smell so sweet. My hair was not always pretty.

I had no silk ribbons.

My homework was not always done. Being smart

and smelling good makes friends. I did not have friends

and this is why. Fourth grade was tough.

And then one day it happened. I met my friend.
Mrs. Marzetta Kerry, my fourth grade teacher was
the most beautiful lady I had ever seen. She looked
like Mama. She smiled like Mama. She hugged
like Mama.

Mrs. Kerry was a good teacher. She was very
smart. She knew what fourth graders needed. She knew
we needed to learn to read well and do math problems.
But she also knew that fourth graders needed friends.
I did not have friends and she knew why.

$\mathcal{S}$ometimes she would take me to a quiet corner and comb my hair and put on a silk ribbon. Then she would look me in the eyes and say, "Glenda, you are Special." She loved me and I knew it. She was my best friend.

As I watched Mrs. Kerry in the classroom, I dreamed of being just like her. To myself I would say, "when I grow up I want to look like that lady....When I grow up I want to talk like that lady.....When I grow up I want to love like that lady."

One day the children at my school were given a chance to be a part of a special program. They would be dancers at a great big park in our city. Teachers chose children they thought would be good dancers and they were sent to the auditorium to try out. Mrs. Kerry picked me.

I was so happy, but I knew that if I was chosen I would not have a pretty dress to dance in. As always, she brushed away my fears by saying "Don't worry Glenda. If you are chosen, I will buy your beautiful dress and drive you to the park."

I joined the other children in the auditorium. When my name was called I went up on the stage and danced my heart out. They chose me. I would dance at the great big park with all the other children.

On that special day Mrs. Kerry took me to her big house. She bathed me with sweet smelling soap. She combed my hair and buttoned me up in the most beautiful white dress I had ever seen.

As she drove me to the park I felt like Cinderella going to the ball.

*A*fter parking the car we ran across the grass holding hands. We were going to meet the other dancers. Then she turned my hand loose. She said, "Hurry Glenda join your friends."

As I ran toward the children, I stopped and turned around to say "thank you." She had made me so happy. She made me feel so special.

Her words to me were "Hurry Precious, you'll be late."

I replied, " but I want to say thank you."

She then said, "Don't say thank you, just dance pretty for me."

That was a beautiful evening. Fourth grade was a

wonderful year. That year I met my life long friend,

my teacher, who stood in for Mama.

The End

ABOUT THE AUTHOR

Glenda Horton Manning is a Sociologist and Consultant who specializes in Family Empowerment. She is married to her high school sweetheart. They have 2 children and 3 grandchildren.

Mrs. Marzetta Hardy Kerry died in Charlotte, North Carolina at age 74.

Often Glenda visited with her teacher who she affectionately called "My Marzetta." Even though Mrs. Kerry suffered from Alzheimer's, she enjoyed long conversations with Glenda as they talked about the old Fairview School where they first met, the principal, Mr. Byers and all their wonderful friends.

Presently, Glenda is an accomplished national Motivational Speaker and CEO of Touch Inc., a Motivational Consultant Training Service. Often she tells her audiences, "I am dancing for Marzetta today!"

OTHER BOOKS BY THE AUTHOR

The Gospel According to Mama - Words To My Children

I Dream of A World

The "Be" Attitudes of Parenting

ORDER FORM

Name:_____

Address:_____

City:_____ State_____ Zip_____

Sales Tax:
Please add 6$\frac{1}{2}$% for books shipped with North Carolina

Shipping:
# of books_____ at $ _14.95_ per book plus $3.95 shipping and handling

Payment: Touch, Inc.
( ) check   ( ) money order   ( ) cashier's check

Mail Payment to: TOUCH, INC.
                    6316 MONTIETH DRIVE
                    CHARLOTTE, NC 28213